# Dad at the Beach

Written by Jill Eggleton

Illustrated by Raymond McGrath

# The people in the book

Dad

The kids

The people at the beach

# The Beach

Dad and the kids went to the beach. Dad put his towel on the sand.

"Look at your towel," said the kids. "It has holes."

"I like my towel," said Dad.

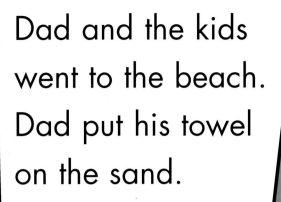

The kids went for a walk.
Dad went, too.
He took the big beach umbrella.

"You can't take that,"
said the kids.

The kids went for a swim.
Dad went, too.
He put big yellow pants
over his swimming togs.

"Your pants are too big,"
said the kids.

"I like big pants," said Dad.
"I look cool!"

The kids are...?

The kids were riding the waves onto the beach.

"I can do that," said Dad.

But Dad's pants were so big, a wave took them off.

"Help," shouted Dad. "A wave took my pants!"

Dad will...?

Dad went under the water to look for the pants.

**No pants.**

The kids went under the water to look for the pants.

**No pants!**

Then Dad saw a dog on the beach.
The dog had Dad's pants in its mouth.

"I can see my pants,"
said Dad.

He got out of the water and
ran after the dog.

What will the dog do
with Dad's pants?

But the dog made
a hole in the sand.
It put Dad's pants in the hole.
And then it put sand
over Dad's pants!

"STOP!" shouted Dad.
"That is not a bone!"

Dad will...?

Dad had to dig his pants up. The kids laughed and laughed.

And the people on the beach laughed, too!

On the way home, Dad and the kids went shopping. Dad got a new towel, a sun umbrella and some new pants!

The End

# Symbols

Dad is…?

Dad is…?

Dad is...?

The kids are...?

# Word Bank

bone

towel

dog

umbrella

pants

wave